By the Author

Novels
The Professionals
Dear Parson
The Laughter in Djakarta
A Revenger's Comedy

Criticism
Proust (Oxford Past Masters)
Hannah Arendt (Penguin Lives of Modern Women)
Critical Times: The History of the *Times Literary Supplement*

Journalism
Feather Reports
The Times: A Year in Nature Notes

As Editor
Oxford Poetry 1952
(with James Price)
The Music of What Happens:
Poems from the *Listener*, 1965-1980

WONDERING ABOUT MANY WOMEN

WONDERING ABOUT MANY WOMEN

DERWENT MAY

GREENWICH EXCHANGE
LONDON

Acknowledgements
Some of these poems first appeared in *Encounter*, the *Observer*, the *Times Literary Supplement*, the *London Magazine*, the *London Review of Books* and *Thames Poetry*.

Greenwich Exchange, London

Wondering About Many Women
© Derwent May

First published in Great Britain in 2011
All rights reserved

Printed and bound by imprintdigital.net
Cover design by December Publications
Tel: 028 90286559
Cover image: Young Woman in Cafe Hawelka, Vienna, circa 1956
© Mary Evans Picture Library/Imagno

Set in Minion 10/12

Greenwich Exchange Website: www.greenex.co.uk

Cataloguing in Publication Data is available
from the British Library

ISBN: 978-1-906075-62-0

to Yolanta

CONTENTS

Wondering About ...

Wondering about many women – all
Who looked at me and fell into my care;
Wondering about what they used to feel,
How much they laughed, how much they chose to bear;
Whether any sigh to think of me still,
If they fix a year by our affair.

Wondering about the one who by a kiss
Set all that was really meant in train,
Laid up for me and for herself
Strange shares of tenderness and pain,
And will not see another take her place
– As now she steps in through the door again.

THE DRESSING-GOWN

I lay in the cool light
As it gleamed on the silk paper,
Calm after the night,
Watching the motes caper
Across the small pane
Through one sunny taper.

The walls of that high room
Shone as never before.
The girl got out of bed,
Picking up from the floor
Her red dressing-gown
As she went towards the door.

As she put it on
She held the window-frame.
My eyes fastened on her,
The sun did the same,
And all the walls around
Burst into harsh flame.

A Girl Asleep

Without so much as touching her
Or opening my eyes
Or hearing any sound from her
I feel her where she lies

And know beneath the silent skin
The blood goes flying warm,
Her heart plays on, while in her breast
Recurs the soundless storm –

Because a jet of living air
Is playing on my arm!
Cooling, it warms me in the dark,
Crowding the bed with calm.

ENEMIES OF LOVE

So many enemies of love: your beauty changing
Like flowers with summer's knowledge into the curved seed;
Dawn dew on new fields; every dusk's
Invasion of fireflies carrying dance into the trees;
Dusk from behind bringing its old embrace,
Each kiss known on the bent nape;
White hands of the sunny ocean falling
Back from this empty beach where the rocks meet.

So many enemies of love; and you and I
Agents of all: pride demanding your beauty
(Darkness hating the wounding touch of light);
Strange consent to body's restless seeking,
And fear that comes always with love's disarming –
Only less sure than love, in this ghostly fight.

Five Minutes Past

Five minutes past I hit the clock – its wrinkled lips
Opened to murmur that you would not come.
Closed again now, their old indifference tells me
I have not even the clock besides myself to hate.

SIGNS OF FEELING

One man in a large room: writing.
A bus passes, a manhole clinks; and then
The night rubs down to silence again.
Sleep billows out from the children's room: inviting.

He sits on in the large room: waiting.
He casts around for signs of feeling; and then
Abruptly writes a line or two again.
He remembers seeing another sign: hating.

Coming Back

Hurrying – hanging back – along the street.
Light from the house lost in the yellow glare.
Light in the hall. A hand on the cold rail:
The palm tense. Silence on every stair.

Smiling faces in frames – taut and still.
A sigh begins to tremble in the air.
The air flies past. Black through an open door:
The silence of sleep! – and her dark head lying there.

The Ginger Cat

The ginger cat on the curtained bed
Only purred,
Beside her, men cried, went mad, went blind
Or died.
But till long after the last train had gone past
She only, slightly, stirred.

TODAY

I sometimes lie in the darkness
Glad there is nothing I can see
To blot the pictures in my memory:
Sunlight in a fallen tree
Where I hung on the wilting branches;
Woodlarks circling in the sky
Or folding like a bell into the heather;
Blue light hardening to die

Out of which there hurry faces,
Lips, smiles, a sudden frown,
A body white in the bracken,
Raindrops where the leaves lay brown,
Water, pavements, water,
A fence where the starlings preen –
I compel them through my memory,
Never asking what else might have been.

And then I go down to the children
And watch them sleeping in their room.
Will today be quite forgotten?
I summon it out of the gloom
And wish it into their memories
For a day I shall never see …

Is it me I want them to remember?
What am I remembering but me?

THE WALK

I took the three children over the hill.
All that morning the sun was like a curtain
Wrapping pine and birch in its yellow folds.
We followed a gold woodpecker through the trees
Gazing after the marks it left on the sunlight
But it led us across a ditch at the edge of the wood;
And we found ourselves in shining ebony stubble
Where we stood together up on a bale in the field.

The older boy, the stranger to me, did not notice
That, during that same summer perhaps, he had learned
To look at the wood through the same eyes as I could:
Marking the sights with the names of common ownership,
Already touching the curling bark on the trees
With the light touch of a man on his daughter's hair.
He, too, came along like a child,
Following me where he always could have led.

It was different with my nephew. At first I wished
That this had been spring, the boughs under fresh loads.
But everything I showed him was pure beginning –
Nothing moved to which he would not give heed.
The trees leaved afresh for him on their trunks,
Holes in the sandy ground breathed like rabbits,
While out of every withering purple bramble
Old nests glided, winged, into his head.

As for the youngest, who knows what she may have seen?
When I lifted her up over pools, she felt her feet
Glide through the stiff grass-tops; she felt her hand
Like an egg in the nest of my giant glove. She heard
Myriad sounds. And certainly she stared at
The brilliance in which she floated like a thread,
Though perhaps she thought it only another creation
Of her mother and father at home over their tea.

I was allowed to choose the way. And the light
Seizing the one who looked most like the leader
More greedily and more thoroughly ravished me –
Though all the time I knew that it was the children
Conducting the light. I needed niece and nephew
And little boy who was older than he thought,
And really it was I who happily got them
To climb up with me on top of that bale in the field.

A Midsummer Night's Dream
in Regent's Park

And what will they remember when
They wake, like Bottom, from their dream?
Will they believe they laughed like this?
And will their restless bodies seem
The same that settled here like dew
Along the benches, in a trance
Of hope and wonder, while old Puck
Led the four lovers through their dance?

The treetops rustle, and the sky
Darkens around a haughty moon.
Cartoon words on homespun lips
Float through the night in their balloon.
Titania curses Oberon
And up the loyal fairies leap.
Within a wood within a wood
The four enchanted lovers sleep.

And will these children ever think
Again about this leaf-lit scene –
Even a single turning branch
Glimmer in their darker green?
Perhaps one moment when the sky
Was dropping dusk light from above
Will touch their eyes with tenderness
Before another night of love.

A Child in the 80s

'Daddy, how old is Groucho Marx?'
  'Sorry, dear boy, he's dead.'
'Gosh! And Chico? Oh yes, and Harpo?'
  'Dead. All of them dead.'
'Daddy, is Lassie very old?'
  'Dogs die young, you know.'
'Will Hay's good! Is he dead too?'
  'Thirty years ago.'

'Daddy, if Elvis comes this way
  Can we go and hear him?'
'Elvis stays in Memphis now,
  Blue carnations near him.'
'Sossidge is on again tonight.'
  'That was Joyce Grenfell, eh?'
'Was? Oh, Daddy, did she die?'
  'Just the other day.'

This is immortality
  Never dreamed of yet:
Life because a child sits by
  A television set.
'Gary Cooper's good on horses.'
  'That was his last ride.'
'Disney must be very rich.'
  'Was, until he died.'

But the child who's sitting there
  Starts to love each day
People who at natural breaks
  Death will take away.
'John Wayne – Bogey – Errol Flynn –
  Are they full of lead?'
'Darling, it wasn't quite like that –
  But all of them are dead.'

CHRISTMAS POEM

Small girls are the tenants of Christmas: when now
Quiet in their pews each stands at the crib's side
And folds a coverlet in prayer over the crying Child,
Happy and awed, and alone in a new pride.

Later in their pain they will not remember
(Turning to one comfortless standing by)
How each ravished smile was told on a smaller face;
But the ceremony will proceed, until with torn eye,

Old, they will return to where the crib still stands,
Seeing there a child whose features will be known
But passed beyond every dream of return now
To where they stoop; and again they will be alone.

EPITHALAMION

The sombre monuments are stirred:
London's anguished staring sky
Breaks, in a smile of birds.
Now that all wakes with this joy
Loosing each banner and tree,
City's founding stream
Lead the melody –
                    Dark Thames, sleep not.

O soft may the air be
That carries them from this day
And soft to all rough dream
Their fingers' touch;
While in passion's changing world
Passion ever stay
And while they sleep
                    Dark Thames, sleep not.

Vanishings

Our parents stand and stretch their arms
    Over our first horizon.
We sing and grow and find ourselves
    Breathing with them in unison.
But then their loving arms grow tired;
    We hear discordant breath.
They bend to the horizon's line
    And vanish into death.

Our children fly into the field,
    Peck and grow and sing.
They sleep beneath our outstretched arms,
    Futures for the asking.
But then they rise and wheel away,
    Wingtips like a knife.
Smaller in the sky they get,
    And vanish into life.

TEMPLE OF DREAMS

When one began one chose between the dreams,
And never seemed to feel the lightest hand
Pushing one this or that way; all was choice;
And will was both as fluid as the sand
And powerful as the sea. These were the themes:
Guilt, and incomprehension and its guilt,
From which one learned to make each better choice.
And so the temple of the dreams was built.

This temple was oneself. It had its lights,
Its elegant embrasures and a floor.
Some of the rooms were dark on certain nights.
Here was a violet stain, a swollen door.
But for a while it grew and gave its pleasure.
It seemed to be one meaning of the world,
Properly measured out for work and leisure,
While dreams grown colourless around it swirled.

But choice had gone. The temple, now complete,
Was what it was. For dreams there was no purchase.
Nothing occurred of guilt or revelation:
Polish waxed proud on every shining surface.
And if men challenged one about the good,
One pointed to the temple one had made.
That was the marble end of all one's labours.

Will still could pull it down; but is afraid.

A February Memory

The black ducks were riding out on the wind-waves
That February morning; still I could see
That the water darts pooling on their backs,
The wind falling like branches from a tree,
Did nothing to dispel the black ennui
With which they waited for the time to pair.
So I shouted and clapped the hollows of my hands
And with gratitude they sprang on to the air.

The Djakarta girl who cooked for me every day
Looked like those birds: she squatted on the floor,
Eyes dull as the water in a pail,
Mouth lying flat on her rounded jaw,
While across the kitchen the sun, yellow and raw,
Slotted through the banana trees in a rain –
Till I called for the sweet, jungle-spotted tea
And at the sound she sprang into smiles again.

On Monte Carlo station one afternoon,
My father told me, he saw a sleepy man
Waiting to take his ticket. When he got there
His ticket was levered up by a bulgy hand
And corresponding left-hand fingers began
To tear off the outward portion. They got half-way,
Then stopped. And the bulgy left hand fell forward again
With the flapping ticket left for the Last Day.

But I distract myself with my father's story.
Indolence is not ennui; and this afternoon
I am like the birds and that girl, not the ticket-collector:
Much travelled in mind and body, sitting down in a room
In Warsaw, now; some men on the roof with broom
And iron spikes breaking the frozen snow.
It shuffles to the gutter, and icicles glint
Dropping with it down to the courtyard below.

A boy shouts down there; the snow thuds.
Alone, without desires, my mind goes back
To the boy I was fifteen years ago,
Slipping through rhododendrons down to a lake,
Listening whether the wind carried a quack;
The bored birds out on the water's bare
Shining surface; and when I clapped my hands
How with gratitude they leaped on to the air!

A BOY IN THE FIELDS

Holes in the hedge are patched with birds
Gazing at the reddening day.
Sunlight already seems asleep
Seen on the sorrel in the hay.

And through the hay a boy will come
Staring till it stains his eye
Over the fields, with the birds,
Out at the dropping evening sky.

Everything is so unloosed
In a smoky golden sea –
So near the senses – that he feels
The scene is his tranquility.

And roams about the fields with joy,
With a careless owner's pride,
Knowing there is not a mood
That the yellowing grasses hide.

Till suddenly his eye is caught
By a shadow, or a stain:
One dark hollow in the hay
Where two lovers must have lain.

The birds fly from the hedge, and in
A rocking circle start to rave,
Lipping the air with broken notes,
Filling the sky with one black wave.

CLOUDS

Wanting to be a cloud –
It's because they never stop,
Stop moving, changing shape:
Acting, up at the top,
And hurried from within,
So that they never falter,
Never hang their heads
At any sky-blue altar.

Here, it's hard to see –
Hard to be seen, as well.
Everything changes round one.
A shape looms up like a bell
That fades before it rings;
You stretch your hand to crowds
Who turn to nobody.
                              Just
As it must be, up in the clouds.

SKIES

When skies are different shades of grey –
A trap, with low clouds running through –
Seen from a window, yellow-lit,
Some stretch will always seem like blue.

We snatch at every chance of hope,
We see it, we believe it's real:
That must be where the sky beyond
Glints with the tender blue of steel.

But then it's overcast, and then
The shrouded heavens close like night.
We falter, acquiesce – until
The rain leaps up, in streaks of light.

After a Little Stillness

Not that it was not a shaking of the pines:
Not that it was not a leaf upon the wind.

But the wind dropped; and after a little stillness
There was new lemon-light on the warm stones,
Warm trickles of air stirring small shadows,
While a bird was attracted from rock to rock.

Not that it was a visionary landscape –

This was a sight one had
Not seen before.

AUTUMN LEAVES

The leaves come breaking in, some black, some gold.
I rush at them, my body like a broom –
And like a bird, and like one crossing over
To the other side.

This is a sudden pleasure for a man,
Being offered such a violent thing to do,
Just down on a windy morning; all in the space
Of a long stride.

Butting against them is only for the sake
Of touching them; and lowering closed eyes
In the hope that lids may feel this swift spray
Of an unseen tide.

But then, without moving, one is back again
(An unfelt, backward flight) where the air is clear.
Tasks the same, pleasure over, dropped leaves making
No 'other side'.

I lean like a broom-handle by the wall,
Dreams of order pressing their intense
Claims again; while into other doorways
The leaves ride.

LAWN AND LEAVES

On the wind, the leaves come down like birds
Flocking to a lawn where the grass is green and bent
As though, like the birds, they will find in the mud traces
A source of life that will help them through till spring.

But they cling to the mud, and the rain beats hard upon them.
The lime leaves slowly crumble; the leathery plane leaves
Dance on their points for a while, then glide, then drop.
The grass is still. With leaves' help, it will see the spring.

MARCHING OR DYING

Time is a spendthrift. See how he dismays
Those prudent men who calculate their coinage!
Summer's entire parade – the drilling trees
Green-jacketed; and all this autumn carnage.

Also in the leafless season he's a lavish
Outlay. In the sky he mints and scatters
Silver on the lakes and branches. There's no profit.
Branches crack. Ice cracks beneath the skaters.

Snow-bowed syringa, and the petalled pools
Under and afterwards: each one is his doing.
Fear no new conflict. We may use his banners –
Bold in the day's province marching or dying.

POSSESSIONS

This is a poem about having.
Pressing of things against the senses.
Fire and water in the fingers.
Fast colour on the retina.
In the red seas of the body
Surging prow and drifting anchor.
Talk of certain men. For one,
Lawrence knew what is always there.

Lawrence knew what is always there,
What once known cannot be forfeit,
Only out of time augmented:
Knowing himself thus unassailable.
Yeats, for another, knew possessions
Firm as gashes on a tree trunk.
Mind in its adventures using
Sense creating the terrain.

Sense creating the terrain:
Under that superb earth-fountain
Fiery winds for ever playing;
Mind indulging its own comment
And attaching its own coolness.
Not a poem about wanting,
Not a poem about believing,
This is a poem about having.

TRIOLET

The poets gather in the room,
Watching the looks on every face.
They feel the close approach of doom,
The poets. 'Gather in the room!'
The hostess cries, 'I'll have no gloom!
Art and pleasure, fill this place!'
The poets gather in the room,
Watching the looks on every face.

To a Badly-Taught Student

who tried hard to write a thesis on Romanticism, but could not
understand 'why poets used rhymes, etc.'

This student, like all others, in the mud
Should first of all get down upon his arse,
Take his eyes off the sky and look around,
Play with the mud a bit. If his whole class
Squats down and wallows about, that'll do no harm,
They'll come to see mud's different from glass,
Or grass or brass. And so perhaps they'll learn
What can be made from it, and slowly pass
From building-games to useful building.
                                                    Well!
At least it will be better than this farce

In which he's taught to look up at the sky
And make mud patterns there. Forced to the trick,
He gropes for mud and hurls it in the air.
He cannot understand why it won't stick.
Professors stand around him everywhere
Who've learned to throw the mud up with a flick
And slick and quick. Faster, harder they go
Making their patterns, till the air's so thick
With mud, the boy is dizzy.
                                        And it rains down
So foul, you'd think the sky was being sick.

KNOWLEDGE

For some there is no knowledge,
Only the drifting of the air,
A thread rising and glinting,
The dew matt on the pear –
Days an estuary garden
Where the air and the water fly
Like swallows lightly turning
In blue tendrils till they die.

Others acquire knowledge –
Dawdling as the world runs by,
Firm in line and outline,
Pressed into the palm of the eye.
But unloved, unregarded,
As day replaces day,
It accumulates like old papers
And then is thrown away.

For a few, knowledge is restless,
Crying out, 'I am rare',
Asking the imagination
To take it into care
And to lift it with the gesture
That beauty rests upon
So that the cry is sounding
After the few have gone.

The next station is Camden Town, Bank branch. This train terminates at Morden via Bank
Amen

This station is Camden Town, Bank branch. Change here for southbound Northern Line services to Kennington via Charing Cross, and Northern Line services to Edgware
Amen

The next station is Euston, Bank branch. Upon arrival the last set of doors will not open. Customers in the last carriage please move towards the front doors to leave the train
Amen

This station is Euston, Bank branch. Change here for southbound Northern Line services to Kennington via Charing Cross, Victoria Line, and mainline intercity and suburban rail services
Amen

The next station is King's Cross St Pancras
Amen

This station is King's Cross St Pancras
Amen

The Lord be with you
And with thy spirit.

An Hour Ago

An hour ago, under steel skies, with a Dutch missionary,
Laughing at a linguistic view of 'God'.

Javanese girls, laughing under their baskets:
'What strange faith passes there?'

And now in a stinking hotel bathroom, a stained ceiling above,
Knocked by cold water into song, I find myself singing
A hymn my father sang nights now beyond number,
Sitting between my sister's bed and mine, when we had said
We could not sleep for empty heads.

By A Foreign Estuary

The brown water slaps against the pier
And the net on the long pole falls again –
Rises and falls, always empty, as the man with the scooter
Passes the long afternoon expecting nothing.
Voices and sounds, a gull on the small waves,
Keeping the spot where the tide rises and falls.

So, slowly, the strange becomes familiar,
The seeking mind resting as it seeks.
I came here in hope of the new, yet this afternoon
I am loth to move on.
Sand and pines, a bay beyond, a mast tilting –
Sudden arrest of all desire to know.
Yet the eye turns to the pines, the hidden craft;
And in the sunset colours one will go.

Resting again, the sand warm on the palm.
Beyond the boat, the water stretches orange
And the distant shore is white.

White peace beyond the foam!
Does it speak of the new, or does it speak of home?

In the Forest

The man went through the forest as
The leaves ran up the trees
And everywhere the warblers sang
Until they clogged the breeze.

He lay down and he rolled about
In grass as thick as hay
And laughed until he tired himself
And then went on his way.

But suddenly a grey beech tree
Was standing in his track
And as he turned aside to pass
A murmur drove him back.

It was the muttering of the tree
Addressed direct to him.
'You love the leaves on every twig,
The birds on every limb,

'But we in lines in silence rise
And under every sky
Are sealed in silence in our bark
Until we fall or die.

'Our mingling branches never feel
The others as they touch
And not a tree in all this wood
Knows other trees for such.'

The man stared at the high beech tree
Then at the trees around
And saw the speechless forest that
Possessed this fertile ground,

Then quick beneath the silent boughs
That over him had stirred
Holding his forearm to his head
Went on without a word.